BONJOUR

The ideal introduction to French

Dominique Debney

Illustrated by Lorna Kent

Headway · Hodder & Stoughton

Notes for parents

It is common knowledge that learning a foreign language is no easy task, and the sooner one starts, the better.

Bonjour is a lively, practical introduction to French for five to eight year olds. It aims to make learning French exciting, easy and fun.

You do not need to know any French yourself in order to help your child. There is a French/English vocabulary at the back of the book for your reference, but avoid translating whole sections into English.

Each spread in the book covers a particular phrase or topic, building up vocabulary as it goes along.

On the left-hand page of each spread, there is a short piece of dialogue. Encourage your child to read it through several times, and to look carefully at the pictures in order to understand it. If you have the cassette, let your child listen to the dialogue being spoken while looking at the book. Encourage him or her to repeat the words after the cassette and even to act out some of the characters. Join in!

On the right-hand page there are fun activities which help your child practise the words and phrases of the dialogue. Check that your child understands how to do each activity. You may prefer to let your child tackle the activities alone, or you can both work through them together. There are extra activities on the cassette to accompany each spread.

The set of cards in the middle of the book can be cut out and used to play a variety of games while practising the French you and your child will have learnt. Here are a couple of suggestions for games to play.

Pairs
Spread out all the cards face down. One by one, players turn two cards over and name the objects on them in French. If they form a pair, the person can keep them and have another go. (Allow only one extra go each time.) The winner is the person with the most pairs at the end.

The pairs are as follows:
un garçon – une fille; une limonade – un jus d'orange; une glace – des bonbons; un chien – un chat; une voiture – un vélo; un ballon rouge – un ballon jaune; un pantalon – une robe; des chaussettes – des chaussures; un chapeau de soleil – des lunettes de soleil.

Give us a clue!
Put the cards face down. Players take it in turns to select a card and mime an activity related to the object on the card – for example, eating (une glace), driving (une voiture), drinking (un jus d'orange). The winner is the first person to call out the object in French.

Some 'dos and don'ts'

- **Don't** rush your child and expect him or her to remember everything.
- **Don't** get upset if your child makes a mistake or finds something difficult. Remember that learning a language requires a lot of practice and repetition.
- **Don't** insist on perfect pronunciation or flawless grammar. It will put your child off.

- **Do** keep every session with the book fairly short, although this will depend on the age and concentration of your child. Between a quarter and half an hour is usually about right.
- **Do** encourage your child to speak French as well as to listen to it and read it. Have a go at speaking yourself!
- **Do** try and use what has been learned whenever possible, for example by saying 'bonjour' rather than 'hello' and 'merci' rather than 'thank you'.
- **Do** adapt the activities in the book and add some of your own, introducing some more vocabulary – food and drink are always popular.
  Above all,
- **Do** make sure both you and your child enjoy learning French!

Good luck!

Bonjour!

What are these people saying?
Draw a line from the words to the right speech bubble.

Ton nom

Help the children say what their names are.

Je m'appelle Nadine.

Je m'appelle _____.

Michelle

Je m'appelle _____.

Je m'appelle _____.

Nadine

Je m'appelle _____.

Philippe

Sylvie

Nicolas

Je _____ _____.

Laurent

Franck

Je _____ _____.

Je _____ _____.

Draw yourself:

Sophie

Et toi? Comment tu t'appelles?

Je m'appelle _____.

7

Tu habites où?

What would the children below answer if you asked them

- what their names are
- if they are English or French
- where they live

Je m'appelle _____.
Je suis _____.
J'habite à _____.

Je m'appelle _____.
Je suis _____.
J'habite à _____.

LONDRES

BRISTOL

ERIC

Charlotte

PARIS

Claude

Je m'appelle _____.
Je suis _____.
J'habite à _____.

Je m'appelle _____.
Je suis _____.
J'habite à _____.

BORDEAUX

Claire

Et toi ?
Tu habites où?

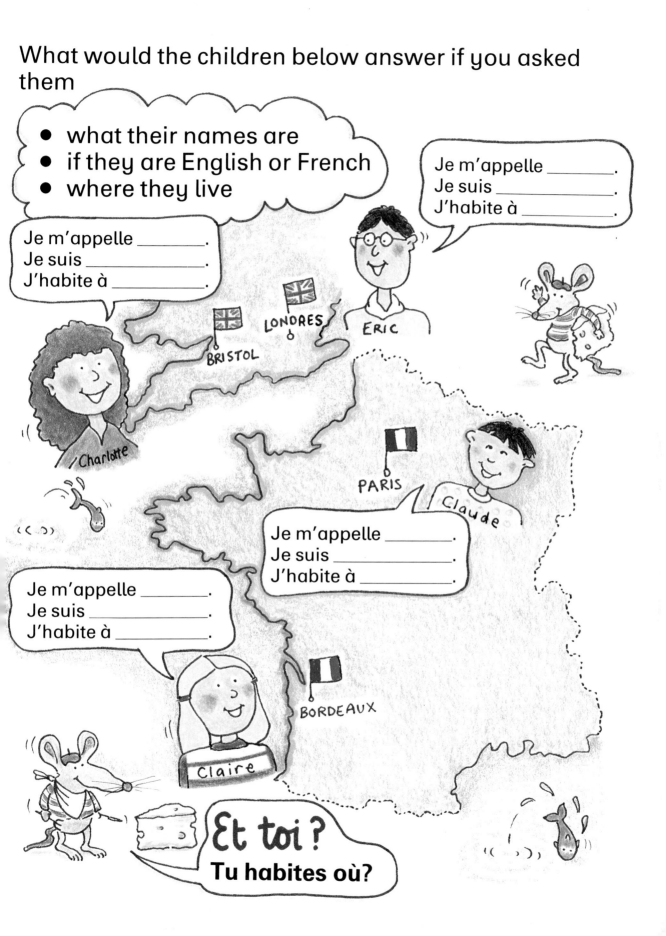

Les nombres

1 un **2** deux **3** trois **4** quatre **5** cinq **6** six **7** sept **8** huit **9** neuf **10** dix

> Il y a combien d'enfants?
> Combien de bébés?
> Combien de filles?
> Combien de garçons?

> 1, 2, 3, 4, 5, 6, 7, 8, 9, 10 enfants.
> 1 bébé. 1, 2, 3, 4 filles.
> 1, 2, 3, 4, 5 garçons.

How many can you see?

d___ maisons

d___ fleurs

q___ voitures

s___ ballons

___ enfants

q___ filles

u___ vélo

___ garçons

u___ ballon

11

Ton âge

Help the children say how old they are.

Charlotte is 2 years older than Claire.
What does she say?

J'ai 7 ans.

J'ai ___ ans.

Paul is 1 year younger than Claude.
What does he say?

J'ai 6 ans.

J'ai _____.

J'ai 9 ans.

Et toi?
Tu as quel âge?

What will Christine say next birthday?

How old will you be next birthday?

Les animaux

Chante avec nous.

Bruits d'animaux

Mon gros chien fait ouah - ouah
Mon oi - seau fait cui - cui

Mon p'tit chat fait mia - ou
Mon poi - sson fait ....

Mon ser - pent fait sss - sss

Mon po - ney fait clip - clop

Mon gros chien fait ouah - ouah

Mon p'tit chat fait mia - ou

Link the animals to their names.

sss-sss

cui-cui

l'oiseau   le chien   le serpent

le poisson   le poney   le chat

clip-clop   miaou   ouah-ouah

Encore des animaux

The children have brought their pets to show us.
Help them to say what their pets are.

J'ai un lapin.

J'ai un _____.

J'ai un _____.

_____.

_____.

_____.

J'ai une _____.

Et toi ?
Tu as un animal
à la maison?

17

Ta famille

voici
ma sœur

voici
mon frère

Voici papa   voici maman   et ça, c'est moi!

Tu as des frères et des sœurs?

Oui, j'ai un frère.

Moi, je suis fille unique.

J'ai une sœur. Et toi Philippe?

J'ai deux frères et une sœur. Et toi Tom?

Je suis fils unique.

Help the children say how many brothers and sisters they have by filling in the gaps in the speech bubbles.

Les couleurs

bleu
rouge
blanc
vert
jaune
rose
marron
violet
noir
gris
orange
blanc

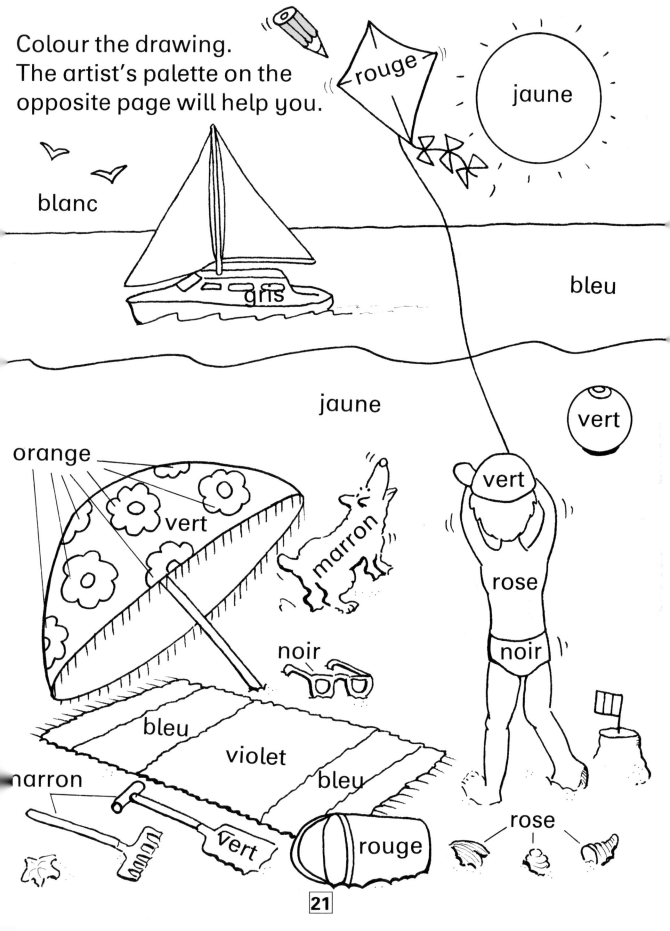

Colour the drawing.
The artist's palette on the opposite page will help you.

rouge

jaune

blanc

gris

bleu

jaune

vert

orange

vert

marron

vert

rose

noir

noir

bleu

violet

bleu

narron

vert

rouge

rose

21

Les vêtements

un chapeau jaune

un short vert

une jupe rouge

un pantalon gris

une robe noire

une chemise bleue

un tee-shirt violet

un pull-over blanc

Nadine et Tom sont déguisés!

Je porte la robe de maman.

Je porte le pantalon de papa.

Nadine, tu portes une chaussette rose et une chaussette orange!

Tom, tu portes une chaussure verte et une chaussure noire!

Hi! hi! hi!

Nicolas

Michelle

Philippe

Sophie

Help these people say what they are looking for. The list below will help you.

chapeau . chaussettes . chaussures . jupe . pantalon . pull-over . robe

J'ai faim, j'ai soif

Who is hungry and who is thirsty?

Follow the maze to find out whether the children want something to eat or drink. Help them say what they want, and whether they are hungry or thirsty.

Je veux un _____.
J'ai _____!

Je veux une _____.
J'ai _____!

Je veux un _____.
J'ai _____!

Je veux un _____.
J'ai _____!

Et toi?

Tu as faim?
Tu as soif?
Qu'est-ce que tu veux?

Start with 'Je veux . . .'

S'il vous plaît, merci

What are these people saying? Draw a line from the words to the right speech bubble.

Merci Monsieur.

Un jus d'orange, s'il vous plaît.

Voilà!

Une glace, s'il vous plaît.

Voilà!

Merci Madame.

16 seize 17 dix-sept 18 dix-huit 19 dix-neuf 20 vingt

Help the children ask the price of what they want.
Tell them the price.

ARTICLES DE PLAGE

CHAPEAUX DE SOLEIL

BOUÉES

c'est combien?

PELLES

_____?

_____?

BALLONS	12 F
SEAUX	18 F
VOITURES	15 F
LUNETTES DE SOLEIL	13 F
PELLES	14 F
CHAPEAUX DE SOLEIL	20 F
BOUÉES	16 F

Et toi ?
Qu'est-ce que tu veux? C'est combien?

29

Le temps

JUILLET
Aujourd'hui il fait du soleil.
Oui, il fait chaud!
Aujourd'hui il neige.
DÉCEMBRE
Oui, il fait froid!
AVRIL
Aujourd'hui il pleut.
OCTOBRE
Aujourd'hui il fait du vent!

Help the children find what they need.
The first one has been done for you.

Il pleut

Il fait froid

Il fait du soleil

Il neige

Il fait chaud

Vocabulaire

à	to, at
âge	age
un an	a year
anglais	English
un animal	an animal
s'appeler	to be called
aujourd'hui	today
au revoir	goodbye
un ballon	a ball, balloon
un bateau	a boat
un bébé	a baby
bonjour	hello, good morning
une bouée	a rubber ring
un chapeau	a hat
un chat	a cat
(il fait) chaud	(it's) hot
une chaussette	a sock
une chaussure	a shoe
une chemise	a shirt
un chien	a dog
un cochon d'Inde	a Guinea pig
combien?	how much, how many?
comment?	how?
un croque-monsieur	a ham and cheese toastie
déguisé	in fancy dress
un enfant	a child
(j'ai) faim	(I'm) hungry
une fille	a girl, daughter
un fils unique	an only child (boy)
une fleur	a flower
français	French
un frère	a brother
(il fait) froid	(it's) cold
le fromage	cheese
un garçon	a boy
un gâteau	a cake
une glace	an ice cream
gros	large, big
habiter	to live
il	he, it
le jambon	ham
jaune	yellow
je, j'	I
un jouet	a toy
une jupe	a skirt
un jus d'orange	an orange juice
le, la, les	the
Londres	London
Madame	Mrs, Madam
mais	but
une maison	a house, home
maman	mummy
merci	thank you
moi	me
Monsieur	Mr, Sir
ne . . . pas, n' . . . pas	not
il neige	it's snowing
un nom	a name

non	no
une orange	an orange
où?	where?
oui	yes
un pantalon	trousers
papa	daddy
parler	to speak
une pelle	a spade
petit	little, small
il pleut	it's raining
un poisson rouge	a goldfish
un poney	a pony
porter	to wear
un pull-over	a jumper
quel	what, which
qu'est-ce que c'est?	what is it?
une robe	a dress
salut	hi
un seau	a bucket
un serpent	a snake
un short	shorts
s'il vous plaît	please
une sœur	a sister
(j'ai) soif	(I'm) thirsty
le soleil	the sun
un tee-shirt	a t-shirt
tu, t', toi	you
une tortue	tortoise
un vélo	a bicycle
le vent	the wind
les vêtements	clothes
violet	purple
voici!	here is
voilà	here you are

British Library Cataloguing in Publication Data

Debney, Dominique
   Bonjour! The ideal introduction to French
   I. Title
   448.3

ISBN 0 340 56285 4

First published 1992

Typeset by Wearside Tradespools, Boldon, Tyne and Wear Printed in Hong Kong for the educational publishing division of Hodder & Stoughton Ltd, Mill Road, Dunton Green, Sevenoaks, Kent by Colorcraft Ltd